THE COOK'S COLLECTION
❉
VEGETABLE
DELIGHTS

Author: Annette Wolter
Photography: Susi and Pete Eising, Odette Teubner,
   Rolf Feuz and Karin Messerli
Translated by UPS Translations, London
Edited by Josephine Bacon

CLB 4157
This edition published in 1995 by Grange Books
an imprint of Grange Books PLC, The Grange, Grange Yard, London SE1 3AG
This material published originally under the series title "Kochen Wie Noch Nie"
by Gräfe und Unzer Verlag GmbH, München
© 1995 Gräfe und Unzer Verlag GmbH, München
English translation copyright: © 1995 by CLB Publishing, Godalming, Surrey
Typeset by Image Setting, Brighton, E. Sussex
Printed and bound in Singapore
All rights reserved
ISBN 1-85627-745-3

THE COOK'S COLLECTION
✳
VEGETABLE
DELIGHTS

Annette Wolter

Grange
BOOKS

Introduction

With more and more people increasing their consumption of vegetables, the demand for appetizing and nutritious vegetable recipes continues to rise. Our greengrocers and supermarkets are bursting at the seams with excellent quality vegetables of countless varieties from all over the world. This book helps you to take advantage of this choice and to incorporate some new ideas into your cooking. You will, of course, also be improving your diet with extra fibre, vitamins and minerals.

Vegetables are best eaten as fresh as possible, but frozen vegetables are better nutritionally than fresh vegetables that have been stored for a long time.

Not only do we now have a vast variety of produce available, but modern cooking methods, borrowed from the East, in particular China, are ideal for the preparation of vegetables. Stir-frying fresh vegetables is quick and easy, and is also nutritionally sound, as the quicker vegetables are cooked, the more vitamins and minerals they retain.

Vegetable cookery is finding a fresh direction, with new flavours and textures combining to create dishes that are both delicious and healthy. This book reflects these changes and offers recipes for many original dishes that use vegetables as a main ingredient, including casseroles, bakes, pasta dishes and salads.

Each recipe serves four, unless otherwise indicated

Sweetcorn Soup with Peas

500g/1lb 2oz peas in the pod
½ tsp salt
1 l/1¼ pints water
400g/14oz canned sweetcorn
2 tsps cornflour
1 tsp sweet paprika
4 tbsps crème fraîche
4 tbsps chopped chives

Preparation time:
30 minutes
Cooking time:
5 minutes
Nutritional value:
Analysis per serving, approx:
• 880kJ/210Kcal
• 8g protein
• 6g fat
• 30g carbohydrate

Shell the peas.• Wash the pods, drain and cook them, covered, in the salted water for 20 minutes.• Purée the corn in a liquidizer or food processor with the liquid from the can or rub it through a sieve.• Drain the pea-pods, reserving the cooking water in a saucepan.• Cook the peas in the reserved liquid for 5 minutes. Add the puréed sweetcorn and more water if required and return to the boil.• Mix the cornflour and paprika with a little cold water. Thicken the soup with this mixture and finally add the crème fraîche. Sprinkle with the chives before serving.

Our Tip: *French beans or strips of sweet pepper may be used instead of peas. In this case, use vegetable stock as a base.*

7

Tomato Soup
with Cheese Dumplings

*750g/1lb 10oz beefsteak
tomatoes
½ tsp each dried thyme and
rosemary
½ tsp each salt and freshly
ground black pepper
Pinch of sugar
Some celery leaves
1 onion
1 tbsp olive oil
1 tbsp flour
Bunch of basil
5 tbsps cream*

For the dumplings:
*200g/7oz full-fat cream cheese
100g/4oz freshly grated
Parmesan cheese
1 egg
2 tbsps flour
Pinch each salt and cayenne*

Preparation time:
1 hour
Nutritional value:
Analysis per serving, approx:
• 1800kJ/430kcal
• 21g protein
• 32g fat
• 15g carbohydrate

Rinse the tomatoes and chop coarsely. Simmer for 20 minutes in a covered saucepan with 750ml/1¼ pints water, the herbs, seasonings and celery leaves. • To make the dumplings, mix together the cream cheese, Parmesan cheese, egg, flour, salt and cayenne. Place in the refrigerator to chill. • Sieve the tomatoes. • Chop the onion and fry until transparent. Dust with flour and fry until light brown. Stir in the tomato purée and simmer for 5 minutes. • Shape the cheese mixture into small dumplings and cook in boiling, salted water for 2 minutes. • Rinse the basil and cut into shreds. • Stir the cream into the soup and season with salt, pepper and sugar. Serve with the dumplings and garnish with basil.

Beetroot Soup

750g/1lb10oz small beetroots
750ml/1¼ pints chicken stock
1 tart apple
Juice of 1 lemon
250ml/4fl oz sour cream
Pinch each salt, freshly ground
black pepper and sugar
1 bunch chives

Preparation time:
40 minutes
Nutritional value:
Analysis per serving, approx:
• 700kJ/170kcal
• 5g protein
• 7g fat
• 22g carbohydrate

Peel the beetroot thinly. Set one aside and chop the others into cubes. •Cook the cubed beetroot in the stock in a covered pan for 20 minutes. •Core the apple, cut into quarters, grate it coarsely and mix with the lemon juice. • Grate the remaining beetroot finely. • Set aside 4 tbsps of the sour cream. • Purée the cooked beetroot in the blender. Mix them with the sour cream. Reheat the soup and season it with salt, pepper and sugar. •Wash and dry the chives and chop finely. • Stir the grated apple and beetroot into the soup. Pour on the remaining sour cream and sprinkle with chives before serving.

Our tip: *The soup is a little richer if you use whipping cream, whipped until semi-stiff, instead of sour cream.*

Pasta Soup with Borlotti Beans

200g/7oz dried borlotti beans
1 small onion
2 garlic cloves
75g/3oz streaky bacon
250g/8oz ripe tomatoes
Handful of fresh parsley
4 tbsps olive oil
About 1l/1¾ pints meat stock
1 tsp celery salt
Generous pinch of black pepper
150g/5½ oz ditali
2 tbsps freshly grated Parmesan cheese

Soaking time:
12 hours
Preparation and cooking time:
1¾ hours
Nutritional value:
Analysis per serving, approx:
• 1890kJ/450kcal
• 19g protein
• 15g fat
• 59g carbohydrate

Cover the beans with twice their volume of water and soak overnight. • Cook the beans in their soaking water in a covered pan for about 1 hour, until soft, then transfer to a sieve, retaining the cooking water. • Meanwhile, peel the onion and the garlic cloves and chop finely. Dice the bacon very finely. Peel and chop the tomatoes. Wash and dry the parsley and chop finely. •Heat the oil in a large pan, then cook the onion and garlic gently until transparent. Add the bacon, parsley, tomatoes and beans, cover the pan and simmer over a low heat for about 20 minutes. • Rub half of this mixture through a sieve. Add the meat stock to the unsieved vegetables, then add enough of the water in which the beans have been cooked to make a total of 1½l/2½ pints of liquid. • Bring the soup to the boil; season with the celery salt and the pepper. • Boil the ditali in the soup until al dente, then stir in the vegetable purée using an egg whisk. Heat through and garnish with the grated Parmesan cheese before serving.

Cheese and Celery Salad

300g/10oz celery heart
Bunch radishes
12 stuffed green olives
200g/7oz mild Gouda cheese
(sliced)
3 tbsps white wine vinegar
½ tsp Dijon mustard
Salt and freshly ground black
pepper
4 tbsps oil
Bunch of mixed herbs, e.g.
basil, dill, parsley, chives

Preparation time:
15 minutes
Standing time:
15 minutes
Nutritional value:
Analysis per serving, approx:
• 1210kJ/290kcal
• 15g protein
• 21g fat
• 6g carbohydrate

Pull off any stringy threads from the celery, but reserve a few of the green leaves for the garnish. Cut the celery sticks into thin slices together with the green leaves. Trim, rinse and dry the radishes. Slice both the radishes and the drained olives. Cut the cheese slices into thin strips. • Mix all the prepared ingredients in a bowl. • To prepare the dressing, mix the vinegar with the mustard, then add the salt and pepper. Pour in the oil and whisk. Pour the dressing over the salad ingredients. • Rinse the mixed herbs in cold water, shake dry and chop finely. Stir into the salad. Cover and leave to stand for 15 minutes. • Serve garnished with the celery leaves. • Serve with French bread and dry white wine.

Our tip: *The taste of celery can easily dominate in mixed salad dishes unless it is used sparingly. If it is really fresh, it will keep in the salad drawer of the refrigerator for up to two weeks.*

Cheese and Fruit Salad

2 tbsps lemon juice
1 tbsp medium sherry
½ tsp sugar
Pinch ground cinnamon
Salt and freshly ground white pepper
4 tbsps walnut oil
250g/8oz mild Gouda cheese
250g/8oz black grapes
2 pears
50g/2oz walnuts
½ head iceberg lettuce

Preparation time:
15 minutes
Standing time:
15 minutes
Nutritional value:
Analysis per serving, approx:
• 2010kJ/480kcal
• 19g protein
• 31g fat
• 28g carbohydrate

Mix the lemon juice with the sherry, sugar, cinnamon, salt and pepper. Add the oil and whisk. • Remove the rind from the cheese and cut into strips. Rinse and halve the grapes. Remove the grape seeds. Quarter, peel and core the pears and cut into thin slices. Halve the walnuts. • Mix all the prepared ingredients in the marinade. Cover and leave in a cool place for 15 minutes. • Pull the leaves from the lettuce. Rinse and shake dry. • If necessary, season the salad before serving on a bed of lettuce leaves.

Wholewheat Pasta with Mushrooms

500g/1lb 2oz mushrooms
3 onions
1 clove garlic
Salt
30g/1oz butter
Freshly ground white pepper
125ml/4fl oz single cream
250g/8oz wholewheat pasta
twists
3l/5 pints water
3 tbsps dry white wine
1 egg yolk
½ bunch parsley
Bunch chives

Preparation time:
40 minutes
Nutritional value:
Analysis per serving, approx:
• 1890kJ/450kcal
• 15g protein
• 19g fat
• 52g carbohydrate

Rinse and trim the mushrooms. Pat dry and slice thinly. Peel the onions and chop finely. Peel the garlic clove, chop, sprinkle with salt and crush with the blade of a knife. •Heat the butter and fry the onion until soft. Add the mushrooms and garlic and fry gently. Season with the remaining salt and pepper. • Add the cream. Leave the pan uncovered and allow the liquid to reduce over medium heat. • Cook the pasta in salted water for 10 minutes or until al dente. • Pour the white wine into the mushroom sauce. Beat the egg yolk into two tablespoons of the hot sauce, then return it to the pan, stir well and remove from the heat. • Rinse, dry and chop the parsley and chives. Mix the parsley into the sauce. • Drain the pasta in a colander and rinse under hot water. Serve at once on warmed plates. Garnish with the chopped chives.

Spinach Gnocchi

To serve 6:
250g/8oz curd cheese
2 slices stale white sandwich bread
125ml/4fl oz milk
700g/1½lbs spinach
50g/2oz grated Pecorino (or Feta cheese)
50g/2oz freshly grated Parmesan cheese
125g/5oz flour
2 eggs
Salt and freshly grated black pepper
Pinch nutmeg
3l/5 pints water

Preparation time:
1¼ hours
Standing time:
30 minutes
Nutritional value:
Analysis per serving, approx:
• 1220kJ/290kcal
• 19g protein
• 9g fat
• 28g carbohydrate

Leave the curd cheese to drain in a colander. • Cut the crust off the bread and soak in milk. • Pick over the spinach and discard any yellow leaves or hard stalks. Rinse the spinach leaves in a saucepan of water. Drain the water into another pan. Add the spinach and leave for 2 minutes over a high heat. Then drain well. Chop finely. • Mix the Pecorino and the Parmesan cheeses. Reserve half and mix the other half with the flour, eggs and seasoning. Stir in the drained curd cheese, the well-squeezed white bread and spinach. Leave in a cool place for 30 minutes. • Bring the water to the boil in a large saucepan. Use wet hands to shape dumplings from the cheesy dough. Cook in salted water for 7-8 minutes. • Serve the gnocchi on warmed plates, sprinkled with the mixture of grated cheese and knobs of butter.

Spicy Courgette Salad

500g/1lb 2oz courgettes
1.5 l/2½ pints of water
Salt and freshly ground white pepper
Ice cubes
1 onion
4 small, ripe tomatoes
4 tbsps canned diced pumpkin with 1 tbsp juice reserved
2 tbsps herb vinegar
Pinch of sugar
1 small garlic clove
4 tbsps olive oil
2 tbsps snipped chives

Preparation time:
25 minutes
Nutritional value:
Analysis per serving, approx:
• 460kJ/110kcal
• 4g protein
• 4g fat
• 15g carbohydrate

Wash, dry and trim the courgettes. Slice fairly thinly. • Bring the water to the boil and add ½ tsp salt. Blanch the courgette slices for 2 minutes. Drain and refresh in iced water, and drain again well. • Peel and chop the onion. • Wash and dry the tomatoes, and cut into eight. • Chop the pumpkin. • Mix together the vinegar, pumpkin juice and sugar, and season to taste with salt and pepper. Crush the garlic and add to the seasoned vinegar. Beat in the oil. • Place the courgettes, onion, tomatoes and pumpkin in a salad bowl, pour over the dressing and garnish with the chives.

Artichoke Heart Salad

200g/7oz round lettuce
200g/7oz radicchio
100g/4oz lamb's lettuce
2 small onions
200g/7oz canned artichoke
hearts
2 tbsps white wine vinegar
Pinch of sugar
1 large garlic clove
4 tbsps sunflower oil
Salt and freshly ground white
pepper
2 tbsps finely chopped fresh
mixed herbs

Preparation time:
25 minutes
Nutritional value:
Analysis per serving, approx:
• 400kJ/95kcal
• 4g protein
• 5g fat
• 10g carbohydrate

Separate the lettuce and radicchio into leaves, wash and shake dry. Trim and wash the lamb's lettuce and leave to drain. • Peel and thinly slice the onions and push out into rings. • Drain the artichoke hearts and cut into quarters. • Mix together the vinegar and sugar. Crush the garlic and add to the vinegar. Beat in the oil, and season to taste with salt and pepper. • Place the lettuce, radicchio and lamb's lettuce in a salad bowl, and top with the artichoke hearts and onion rings. Pour over the dressing, sprinkle over the herbs and serve immediately.

Caponata

500g/1lb 2oz aubergines
Salt and freshly ground black
pepper
250g/8oz onions
250g/8oz tomatoes
1 small head of celery
75g/3oz stoned green olives
6 tbsps olive oil
1 tbsp capers
2 tbsps sultanas
1 tbsp pine nuts
125ml/5 fl oz white wine
vinegar
1 tbsp sugar

Preparation time:
1½ hours
Cooling time:
2 hours
Nutritional value:
Analysis per serving, approx:
• 880kJ/210kcal
• 5g protein
• 11g fat
• 23g carbohydrate

Wash and dice the aubergines. Place in a colander, sprinkle over 1 tsp salt and set aside for 30 minutes to drain. • Peel and thinly slice the onions and push out into rings. • Skin the tomatoes, and chop finely. • Separate and wash the celery. Chop into 3cm/1-inch pieces. Blanch in a little boiling water for 5 minutes, and drain. • Coarsely chop the olives. • Rinse the aubergines and pat dry. • Heat 4 tbsps of the oil in a pan, and fry the aubergines over a high heat for a few minutes. Remove and drain on absorbent paper. Add the remaining oil to the pan and reduce the heat. Fry the onion rings until translucent. Add the celery and fry for 2 minutes. Add the tomatoes, and cook for 5 minutes. Stir in the olives, capers, sultanas, pine nuts and aubergines. • Season to taste with salt and pepper, add the vinegar and sugar, and simmer for a further 10 minutes until the vinegar has evaporated. Leave to cool completely before serving.

Dandelion Leaves with Cracked Wheat

100g/4oz cracked wheat (bulgur)
1 tbsp soya sauce
2 tbsps red wine vinegar
2 tbsps olive oil
Freshly ground black pepper
150-250g/6-8oz dandelion leaves or young spinach or sorrel
1 red skin onion
150ml/5fl oz natural yogurt
150ml/5fl oz soured cream
2 tsps French mustard
10 stoned black olives
½ tsp sea salt (optional)

Preparation time:
30 minutes
Standing time:
10 minutes
Nutritional value:
Analysis per serving, approx:
• 1390kJ/330kcal
• 8g protein
• 21g fat
• 28g carbohydrate

Place the cracked wheat in a measuring jug and note its volume. Transfer to a saucepan and add twice its volume of boiling water. Boil for about 10 minutes or until all the liquid has been absorbed. Remove from the heat and allow to cool. Transfer to a salad bowl. • Mix together the soya sauce, vinegar and oil, and season to taste with pepper. Pour over the cracked wheat. • Trim, wash thoroughly and drain the dandelion, spinach or sorrel leaves. Chop very finely, and add to the salad bowl. • Peel and quarter the onion, then cut each quarter into thin slices. Add to the salad bowl. • Beat together the yogurt, soured cream and mustard. Stir in the sea salt, if using. Spoon the mixture over the salad. Coarsely chop the olives, mix into the salad and leave to stand for 10 minutes.

Dandelion Leaves with Aduki Beans

150g/5½oz aduki beans
1 bay leaf
2 tsps vegetable stock granules
150-250g/6-8oz dandelion
leaves or young spinach or
sorrel
2 shallots
1 red skin onion
2-3 yellow or red tomatoes
5-6 tbsps red wine vinegar
5-6 tbsps olive oil
Salt and freshly ground black
pepper

Soaking time:
12 hours
Preparation time:
40 minutes
Standing time:
10 minutes
Nutritional value:
Analysis per serving, approx:
• 500kJ/120kcal
• 4g protein
• 5g fat
• 15g carbohydrate

Place the aduki beans in a bowl, cover with 750ml/1¼ pints of water and leave to soak overnight. • Transfer the beans and the soaking water to a saucepan, add the bay leaf and stock granules and boil for 30 minutes or until tender. Drain well, discard the bay leaf and leave to cool. • Trim, wash and drain the dandelion or spinach or sorrel leaves, and chop very finely. • Peel and finely chop the shallots. Peel and quarter the onion, then cut each quarter into thin slices. • Wash and dry the tomatoes, and cut into eight. • Place the beans, salad leaves, shallots, onion and tomatoes in a salad bowl. Beat together the vinegar and oil, and season to taste with salt and pepper. Pour the dressing over the salad, and leave to stand for 10 minutes.

Asparagus Salad with Béarnaise Sauce

2 shallots
1 tbsp white wine vinegar
250ml/9fl oz dry white wine
500g/1lb 2oz white asparagus
500g/1lb 2oz green asparagus
Salt
Pinch of sugar
1 tbsp lemon juice
250g/8oz firm tomatoes
½ cold cooked chicken
2 tbsps chopped fresh dill
3 egg yolks
150g/5½oz butter
Pinch of cayenne pepper

Preparation time:
45 minutes
Nutritional value:
Analysis per serving, approx:
• 3190kJ/760kcal
• 36g protein
• 56g fat
• 16g carbohydrate

Peel and finely chop the shallots. Bring the vinegar and white wine to the boil and add the shallots. Boil until reduced by about a half. Remove from the heat and leave to cool. • Peel the white asparagus from top to bottom and remove the woody ends. Tie all the asparagus spears loosely together, stand upright in a large pan and cover with water. Add 1 tsp salt, the sugar and lemon juice, bring to the boil and cook for 15-20 minutes. • Skin, halve and seed the tomatoes. Dice the flesh. • Skin the chicken, remove the meat from the bones and dice it. • Cut off the top third of each asparagus spear, and cut in half again (use the lower parts and the cooking liquid to make soup). • Combine the diced tomato, asparagus tips, chicken and dill. • Beat the egg yolks into the cooled wine mixture. Melt the butter and, when lukewarm, pour it in a thin stream into the wine mixture, gently stirring all the time. Season the sauce with salt and cayenne pepper, and pour over the salad.

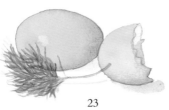

Vegetarian Pasta Salad

3l/5¼ pints water
1 tsp salt
300g/10oz pasta verde (ditali, conchiglie or tagliatelle)
2 green peppers
2 shallots
Small handful of parsley
Handful of chives
150g/5½oz Gorgonzola cheese
3 tbsps vinegar infused with herbs
150g/5½oz crème fraîche
Salt and freshly ground black pepper
1 hard-boiled egg

Preparation time:
40 minutes
Nutritional value:
Analysis per serving, approx:
• 2600kJ/620kcal
• 24g protein
• 31g fat
• 62g carbohydrate

Add salt to the water and bring to the boil. Cook the pasta for about 8 minutes or until al dente. • Quarter the peppers, remove the stalk, pith and seeds, wash and cut into thin strips. Peel the shallots and chop finely. Wash and dry the parsley and chives, then chop finely. • Mash the Gorgonzola and mix it with the vinegar, crème fraîche, salt, pepper, diced shallots and the herbs. Set 1 tbsp chives aside for garnishing. • Shell the egg and chop finely. • Combine the pasta with the strips of pepper, and stir in the cheese sauce. • Serve the salad garnished with the egg and chives.

Pasta and Bean Salad

3l/5¼ pints water
1 tsp salt
300g/10oz pasta (penne or ditali)
250g/8oz French beans
100g/4oz sliced ham sausage
10 green stuffed olives
Handful of parsley
1 onion
2 tbsps mayonnaise
175ml/5fl oz sour cream
2 tbsps red wine vinegar
Salt and freshly ground black pepper

Preparation time:
40 minutes
Nutritional value:
Analysis per serving, approx:
• 2010kJ/480kcal
• 18g protein
• 16g fat
• 64g carbohydrate

Salt the water and bring to the boil. Add the pasta and cook for 8–10 minutes or until al dente. Trim and wash the beans, cut into pieces about 3cm/1¼ inches long, and cook in a little boiling salted water for 15 minutes. Then drain in a colander, reserving about 3 tbsps of the cooking water, and leave to cool. • Cut the ham sausage into strips and slice the olives. Wash and dry the parsley and chop it finely, retaining 1 sprig for garnishing. • Peel the onion, chop very finely and mix with the mayonnaise, sour cream, vinegar, the cooking water and the chopped parsley. • Combine the drained, cooled pasta with the beans, the ham sausage and the olives. • Dress the salad with the mayonnaise dressing, seasoning with salt and pepper.

Tip: Leftovers of roast beef make a good substitute for the ham sausage. Instead of mayonnaise and sour cream, you can use 5 tbsps cold-pressed olive oil to make the salad dressing.

Pancakes with Courgettes in Cream

100g/4oz flour
2 eggs
125-250ml/4-8fl oz mineral water
Salt
400g/14oz courgettes
1 small onion
½ garlic clove
125ml/4fl oz vegetable stock
½ bunch thyme
4 tbsps crème fraîche
2 tbsps butter

Preparation time:
40 minutes
Nutritional value:
Analysis per serving, approx:
• 1100kJ/260kcal
• 9g protein
• 14g fat
• 27g carbohydrate

Mix the flour with one whole egg, one egg yolk and sufficient water to produce a thick batter. Stir in a pinch of salt and leave the batter to rest. • Rinse the courgettes in lukewarm water, dry and chop. Peel the onions and chop. Peel and crush the garlic. • Bring the vegetable stock to the boil. Add the onions, courgettes and garlic. Cover and simmer for about 10 minutes. • Whisk the remaining egg white until stiff and then fold into the egg batter. • Rinse the thyme, shake dry and chop finely. Boil the vegetable stock in order to reduce it slightly. Stir the crème fraîche into the stock. If necessary, season again. Add the thyme, cover, and set aside. • For each pancake, melt half a teaspoon of butter in a small frying pan. Fry the pancakes on both sides, fill with the vegetables and fold over. Serve hot.

Stuffed Aubergines

2 medium-sized aubergines
(600g/1lb 6oz)
½ tsp salt
100g/4oz streaky bacon
2 onions
1 clove garlic
4 tomatoes
200g/7oz button mushrooms
300g/10oz long-grain
rice,cooked
½ tsp each salt and sweet
paprika
¼ tsp each pepper and ground
caraway seeds
1 tbsp chopped parsley
4 tbsps grated Cheddar cheese
375ml/15 fl oz vegetable stock
100ml/4 fl oz natural yogurt
2 tsps cornflour
3 tbsps tomato purée
Pinch of sugar

Preparation time:
30 minutes
Cooking time:
40 minutes
Nutritional value:
Analysis per serving, approx:
• 1680kJ/400kcal
• 13g protein
• 23g fat
• 35g carbohydrate

Halve the aubergines lengthways. Scoop out the flesh, and chop finely. Salt the insides of the aubergines. Dice the bacon. Peel the onions and garlic, and chop finely. Skin the tomatoes and chop finely. Trim the mushrooms, and slice thinly. • Preheat the oven to 200°C/ 400°F/Gas Mark 6. • Fry the bacon in a dry frying-pan until the fat runs. Add the onions, garlic, mushrooms and chopped aubergine and sauté together, stirring occasionally. Add the tomatoes, and cook, covered, for 5 minutes. Mix in the rice; season with the spices and parsley. Stuff the aubergines and sprinkle with cheese: put in a baking dish, pour hot vegetable stock round the aubergines and bake in the oven for 40 minutes. • Soften the cornflour in a little cold water and combine with the cooking liquid, yogurt, tomato purée and sugar in a saucepan. Bring briefly to the boil. Serve the sauce separately.

Macaroni with Broccoli

3 garlic cloves
3 anchovy fillets
1kg/2¼lbs broccoli
2l/3½ pints water
2 tsps salt
200g/7oz macaroni
3 tbsps olive oil
Generous pinch of cayenne pepper
Freshly ground white pepper

Preparation and cooking time:
1 hour
Nutritional value:
Analysis per serving, approx:
• 1380kJ/330kcal
• 18g protein
• 9g fat
• 48g carbohydrate

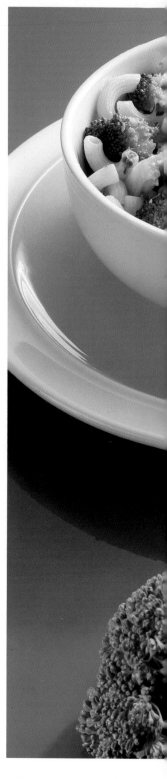

Peel the garlic and chop finely. Rinse the anchovy fillets with water, pat dry and chop finely. Wash the broccoli thoroughly and drain well. Remove the ends of the broccoli stalks and, starting at the bottom, peel to remove the tough outer surface of the stems. Chop the broccoli florets into 5cm/2-inch long pieces (thicker pieces should be cut shorter, so that the cooking time is the same for all pieces). • Add the salt to the water and bring to the boil. Add the broccoli, cover and cook over a medium heat for about 15 minutes. Then drain in a colander, retaining the cooking water. Cover the vegetables and keep them hot. • Bring the water used for cooking the broccoli back to the boil, add the macaroni and cook for about 8 minutes or until al dente. • Meanwhile, heat the olive oil in a small pan. Fry the garlic and the anchovies with the cayenne pepper over a low heat for 15 minutes, stirring frequently. • Drain the pasta in a colander, place in a hot dish, combine with the broccoli and anchovy sauce, cover and leave for 5 minutes to allow the flavour to develop. Stir well before serving. • Season with freshly ground white pepper to taste.

Parsnip Croquettes

600g/1lb 6oz parsnips
125ml/4 fl oz vegetable stock
75g/3oz cracked wheat
2 eggs
1 tbsp yeast extract
½ tsp salt
2 tbsps chopped parsley
5 tbsps safflower oil

Preparation time:
10 minutes
Cooking time:
1 hour
Nutritional value:
Analysis per serving, approx:
• 1365kJ/325kcal
• 8g protein
• 17g fat
• 35g carbohydrate

Peel or scrape the parsnips, wash thoroughly, dry and slice. Cook gently in the vegetable stock for up to 40 minutes or until tender. Add a little more vegetable stock or water if necessary to prevent them from sticking. • Purée the parsnips with the cooking liquid. Sprinkle the cracked wheat over the purée. Add the eggs, yeast extract, salt and chopped parsley and work into a smooth dough. With damp hands, shape the dough into croquettes about the size of your palm. • Heat the oil. Fry the Parsnip Croquettes a few at a time until golden on both sides. Keep the cooked croquettes warm until all the dough has been used. • Lamb's lettuce salad goes well with these.

Our Tip: *When cooked and drained, the parsnips may also be coated in batter as for Chicory Fritters, and fried until golden in plenty of oil. Parsnips cooked slowly in very little liquid and with 2 tbsp single cream added after cooking make a light vegetable side dish.*

Jerusalem Artichoke Fritters

600g/1lb 6oz Jerusalem
artichokes
1 tsp salt
1l/1¾ pints water
½ red pepper
100g/4oz freshly crushed
cracked wheat
½ tsp salt
1 tbsp sweet paprika
2 eggs
5 tbsps safflower oil

Preparation time:
30 minutes
Cooking time:
30 minutes
Nutritional value:
Analysis per serving, approx:
• 1490kJ/355kcal
• 10g protein
• 17g fat
• 40g carbohydrate

Wash, peel and slice the Jerusalem artichokes. Bring the salt and water to the boil. Boil the sliced Jerusalem artichokes for up to 20 minutes or until tender. • Wash the pepper, remove the seeds and white pith, and chop finely. Combine the cracked wheat, salt, paprika and chopped pepper in a bowl. Separate the eggs. Mix the egg yolks and flour together, and add to the other ingredients in the bowl. Drain the Jerusalem artichokes well, chop finely and add to the bowl. Lastly, fold in the stiffly beaten egg whites. • Heat the oil in a frying-pan. Drop the batter into the pan a tablespoonful at a time, and flatten slightly. Fry the fritters until crisp and brown on both sides. Keep the cooked fritters warm until all the mixture has been used up. • Jerusalem Artichoke Fritters taste good with boiled chicken and Brussels sprouts.

Cheese-and-Onion Toast

4 slices thick-cut wholemeal
bread
2 tsps butter
4 large onions
4 tbsps corn oil
150g/5½oz Emmental cheese
Freshly ground black pepper
2 tbsps freshly chopped parsley

Preparation time:
20 minutes
Nutritional value:
Analysis per serving, approx:
• 1400kJ/330kcal
• 13g protein
• 22g fat
• 18g carbohydrate

Toast and butter the bread.
• Peel and chop the
onions. Fry in the hot oil for a
few minutes until soft then
leave on a plate to cool. •
Grate the cheese coarsely and
mix with the cooled onions,
pepper and parsley, reserving a
few sprigs of parsley for the
garnish. Spread the mixture on
the toast. • Melt the topping
under the grill. Sprinkle with
the remaining garnish and
serve the toast whilst hot.

Sauerkraut on Toasted Rye Bread

4 slices rye bread
1 onion
30g/1oz softened butter
Salt
1 tsp paprika
500g/1lb 2oz mild, raw
sauerkraut
4 tbsps sunflower oil
4 tbsps olive oil
1 can of pai-ping
1 tbsp chopped chives

Preparation time:
30 minutes
Nutritional value:
Analysis per serving, approx:
• 1800kJ/430kcal
• 9g protein
• 33g fat
• 21g carbohydrate

Toast the bread. Peel the onion and halve. Chop one half finely and slice the other into thin rings. Mix together the butter, chopped onion, salt and half a teaspoon of paprika. Spread the paprika butter on the toast. • Heat the oven to 180°C/350°C/gas mark 4. •Squeeze the juice from the sauerkraut and loosen the strands with a fork. Mix the remaining paprika with the sauerkraut, sunflower oil and 3 tablespoons of olive oil. Spread this mixture onto the bread. • Add the pai-ping in flakes. Arrange the onion rings in the middle of each slice of bread and sprinkle with the remaining oil. • Place the toast on a baking tray on the top shelf and bake for about 10 minutes. Serve hot sprinkled with chopped chives.

Our tip: Instead of sauerkraut, try the following mixture: three chopped garlic cloves with a tablespoon of finely chopped fresh rosemary and a little lemon juice. Cook 200g/7oz each of aubergine, tomato and courgette plus the garlic mixture in a little oil for 5 minutes, then spread it on the bread. Top with pai-ping flakes and a few drops of oil, then cook in the oven like the sauerkraut toast. Pai-ping is a vegetarian spread with a high fat content. It is available in health food shops.

Layered Wholemeal Bread

To serve 10:
50g/2oz softened butter
50g/2oz margarine
½ tsp salt
250g/8oz Mascarpone (fresh cream cheese)
Generous pinch black pepper
2 tbsps finely chopped chervil
4 tbsps chopped chives
1 small onion
10 black olives
2 tsps tomato purée
1 tsp sweet paprika
50g/2oz grated Emmental cheese
Generous pinch curry powder
Generous pinch turmeric
1 ripe avocado
2 tsps lemon juice
Generous pinch white pepper
Generous pinch herb or celery salt
Dash of Tabasco sauce
400g/14oz wholemeal loaf

Preparation time:
20 minutes
Cooling time:
2 hours
Nutritional value:
Analysis per serving, approx:
• 1590kJ/380kcal
• 25g protein
• 9g fat
• 27g carbohydrate

Blend the butter with the margarine, salt, pepper and 100g/4oz of mascarpone. Mix in the chervil and 2 tablespoons of chopped chives, then divide the mixture into 2 portions. • Peel the onions and chop finely. Stone the olives and slice thinly. Mix the chopped onions and olives into one half of the cheese mixture and then add the tomato purée, paprika and 50g/2oz of the mascarpone. • Add the grated Emmental, curry powder and turmeric to the other half and stir in well. • Purée the avocado flesh and add the lemon juice, the rest of the mascarpone, pepper, savoury salt, Tabasco sauce and the rest of the chives. • Cut the bread into four slices. Spread the red cream thickly over the lower slice and place

34

another slice on top. Spread
this with the curry-flavoured
cream, before covering with
another slice. Spread the green
cream on top and cover with
the last slice. • Leave the
sandwich to cool for 2 hours.
Before serving cut into slices
1cm/½ inch thick.

Baked Cauliflower Florets

375ml/14fl oz water
Salt
1 tbsp tomato purée
Pinch dried fines herbes
50g/2oz fine cornmeal
500g/1lb 2oz cauliflower
florets
50g/2oz Mascarpone
1 tsp each finely chopped
thyme and lovage or ½ tsp
dried mixed herbs
100g/4oz Emmental cheese
(thinly sliced)
2 tbsps chopped chives
Butter for greasing

Preparation time:
45 minutes
Nutritional value:
Analysis per serving, approx:
• 1010kJ/240kcal
• 12g protein
• 14g fat
• 15g carbohydrate

Bring the water to the boil adding salt, tomato purée and fines herbes. Add the cornmeal, whisking constantly. Bring back to the boil, cover and allow to simmer for 10 minutes. Remove from the heat, keep the pan covered and leave to stand for 10 more minutes. • Meanwhile rinse the cauliflower florets, halve if necessary and cook in a little water for 10 minutes. Leave to drain. • Mix the mascarpone and herbs with the cornmeal sauce and, if necessary, add more seasoning. • Heat the oven to 200°C/400°F/gas mark 6. Fill a greased, ovenproof dish with the sauce. Add the cauliflower and top with the Emmental cheese cut into strips. Bake in the oven for 5 minutes. • Serve hot garnished with chives.

Stuffed Chard Leaves

12 large undamaged chard
leaves (300g/10oz)
1 tsp salt
1 large garlic clove
300g/10oz feta cheese
4 egg yolks
200g/7oz crème fraîche
Freshly ground white pepper
4 tbsps white wine
125ml/4fl oz chicken or
vegetable stock
2 tbsps olive oil

Preparation time:
1 hour
Nutritional value:
Analysis per serving, approx:
• 1800kJ/430kcal
• 24g protein
• 34g fat
• 6g carbohydrate

Wash the chard leaves and
shave off some of the
thick white stalks with a sharp
knife. Bring 2 litres/3½ pints of
salted water to the boil. Blanch
the chard leaves for about 10
minutes, drain, dry on a tea
towel and leave to cool. • Peel
and chop the garlic clove, then
crush with the blade of a knife.
Mix the feta cheese with the
egg yolks, 4 tablespoons of
crème fraîche, crushed garlic
clove and some pepper. •
Divide the cheese mixture
between the chard leaves, then
make parcels by folding in the
long sides of the leaves. Place
the parcels in a large pan with
the seam downwards. • Mix
the white wine with the stock
and the olive oil and pour over
the stuffed leaves. Cover and
simmer over a gentle heat for
10 minutes. • Transfer the
stuffed leaves onto a preheated dish and keep warm.
Stir the rest of the crème
fraîche into the stock and
reduce. • Pour the sauce over
the stuffed rolls.

Banitza

500g/1lb 2oz flour
Salt
1 tbsp wine vinegar
About 300ml/12fl oz water
2 eggs
400g/14oz feta cheese
3 tbsps crème fraîche
Handful of fresh dill
1 garlic clove
Freshly ground black pepper
Oil for brushing

Preparation time:
1 hour
Baking time:
30-35 minutes
Nutritional value:
Analysis per serving, approx:
• 3100kJ/740kcal
• 28g protein
• 26g fat
• 96g carbohydrate

Knead the flour with a pinch of salt, the vinegar and enough water to form a smooth dough. Place under a damp tea towel and leave to stand for 1 hour. • For the filling, separate the eggs into yolks and whites. Grate the cheese and mix it with the egg yolks and the crème fraîche. Wash and dry the dill and chop it finely. Peel the garlic cloves, chop finely, sprinkle with a pinch of salt and crush. Beat the egg whites until they form stiff peaks. Stir the dill, garlic and pepper into the cheese, then fold in the egg white. • Heat the oven to 180°C/350°F/Gas Mark 4 and oil a baking tray. • Divide the dough into 10 equal pieces. Roll out two at a time so that each takes up half the area of the baking tray. Lay the first strip on the tray, brush it with oil and place the second strip on top. Meanwhile, keep the rest of the dough covered. Spread a quarter of the filling over the dough on the baking tray. Repeat the procedure until all the dough has been used. Brush the last dough strip liberally with oil. • Bake the banitza in the oven for 30 to 35 minutes, allow to cool briefly, then cut into squares.

Pasta with Celery

500g/1lb 2oz celery
1 onion
1 garlic clove
2 tbsps walnut oil
125ml/4fl oz vegetable stock
125ml/4fl oz dry white wine
400g/14oz pasta (fusilli,
rigatoni or penne)
4l/7 pints water
2 tsps salt
3 tbsps sesame seeds
2 tsps cornflour
3 tbsps single cream
Salt and freshly ground white
pepper

**Preparation and cooking
time:**
40 minutes
Nutritional value:
Analysis per serving, approx:
• 2520kJ/600kcal
• 19g protein
• 18g fat
• 86g carbohydrate

Remove the thicker threads from the sticks of celery and cut off the ends. Retain a few leaves for garnishing. Wash the celery and cut it into thin slices. Peel the onion and garlic and chop finely. Heat the oil in a large pan, add the onion and cook until transparent. Add the celery, pour over the vegetable stock and the wine and cook for 10 minutes. • Cook the pasta in boiling salted water until al dente, then drain and rinse in a colander. • Roast the sesame seeds in a dry pan, stirring all the time, until golden brown. • Mix the cornflour with the cream until smooth; use to bind the celery mixture. Simmer the vegetables for a few more minutes, season with salt and pepper and scatter in the sesame seeds. • Stir the cooked pasta into the vegetables. • If desired, serve with freshly grated Emmental and the same wine as that used for cooking.

Wild Rice Casserole

100g/4oz wild rice
100g/4oz brown rice
1 sprig of thyme
8 basil leaves
750ml/1¼ pints chicken stock
600g/1lb 6oz mixed
mushrooms
50g/2oz streaky bacon
1 onion
1 tbsp oil
Salt and freshly ground black
pepper
2 tbsps chopped parsley

Preparation time:
40 minutes
Cooking time:
1½ hours
Nutritional value:
Analysis per serving, approx:
• 1200kJ/290kcal
• 9g protein
• 11g fat
• 42g carbohydrate

Rinse both varieties of rice in cold water and leave to drain. Bring the stock to the boil, add the rice, thyme and basil, cover the pan and cook for 45 minutes. • Heat the oven to 180°C/350°F/Gas Mark 4. • Wipe the mushrooms and cut the large ones into slices. • Chop the bacon. • Peel and chop the onion. • Heat the oil in a large ovenproof casserole dish. Gently fry the bacon, add the onion and cook until transparent. Add the mushrooms and stir-fry until lightly browned. Season the mushrooms with salt and pepper. • Stir the rice and stock into the mushrooms and cover with a tight-fitting lid. Cook for a further 45 minutes in the oven. • Before serving, sprinkle the rice with chopped parsley.

Mushroom Stew

400g/14oz pork fillet
1 large onion
2 garlic cloves
500g/1lb 2oz oyster
mushrooms
500g/1lb 2oz cup mushrooms
25g/1oz clarified butter
200g/7oz crème fraîche
Salt and freshly ground black
pepper
2 sprigs thyme
750ml/1¼ pints beef stock
2 bunches parsley
1 tbsp balsamic vinegar

Preparation time:
1½ hours
Nutritional value:
Analysis per serving, approx:
• 2000kJ/480kcal
• 28g protein
• 38g fat
• 7g carbohydrate

Rinse the pork, drain, and cut into 1cm/½-inch cubes. • Peel the onion and garlic. Chop the onion. • Cut out any tough sections of stalk from the oyster mushrooms. Rinse and cut into strips. Wipe the cup mushrooms and quarter. • Heat the clarified butter, brown the meat cubes and remove. • Fry the onion until transparent, gradually add the mushrooms and continue to fry until all the liquid has evaporated. • Transfer the pork and mushrooms into a saucepan and add the crushed garlic, followed by the crème fraîche, salt, pepper and thyme leaves. Pour in the beef stock, bring to the boil and simmer for 15 minutes. • Wash the parsley, shake dry and chop the leaves coarsely. Season the pork and mushrooms with the balsamic vinegar and garnish with the chopped parsley.

Pasta Bake with Mushrooms

250g/8oz pasta (macaroni or
spirale)
2½ l/4½ pints water
1 tsp salt
250g/8oz broccoli
250g/8oz mushrooms
2 tbsps oil
1 garlic clove
2 eggs
250ml/8fl oz milk
Pinch each of salt, paprika and
grated nutmeg
125g/5oz grated Parmesan
cheese
1 tbsp each flaked almonds,
sesame seeds and melted butter

Preparation time:
30 minutes
Baking time:
40 minutes
Nutritional value:
Analysis per serving, approx:
• 2600kJ/620kcal
• 32g protein
• 29g fat
• 57g carbohydrate

Cook the pasta in salted water until al dente. • Wash the broccoli. Slice the stems finely, leaving the florets whole. Wipe the mushrooms and slice them finely. Peel the garlic. • Heat 1 tbsp oil and fry the garlic clove briefly. Add the broccoli and cook over a low heat, stirring frequently, for 3 minutes. Then remove from the pan. • Add the remaining oil to the pan. Add the mushrooms and cook until golden . • Drain the pasta. • Heat the oven to 225°C/ 425°F/Gas Mark 7 and butter an ovenproof dish. • Place alternate layers of pasta, broccoli and mushrooms in the dish. Separate the eggs. Beat the egg yolks with the milk, salt, paprika, nutmeg and Parmesan. • Whisk the egg whites until they are fairly stiff, then fold them in. • Pour the egg mixture into the dish. Sprinkle with almond leaves and sesame seeds. Drip melted butter over the top and bake for about 40 minutes.

Bucatini and Aubergine Bake

To serve 6:
3 aubergines
1 tbsp salt
400g/14oz bucatini
4l/7 pints water
1 bunch spring onions
2 carrots
150g/5½ oz celery
Sprig of thyme
125ml/4fl oz olive oil
800g/28oz can tomatoes
100g/4oz grated Feta cheese
150g/5½oz Mozzarella cheese

Preparation time:
1 hour
Baking time:
30 minutes
Nutritional value:
Analysis per serving, approx:
• 3480kJ/830kcal
• 24g protein
• 40g fat
• 91g carbohydrate

Cut the aubergines into slices 1cm/½ inch thick, coat with salt and leave to stand for 20 minutes. • Break the pasta into pieces and cook until al dente. • Peel the onions and carrots, wash the celery and chop all finely. Chop the thyme leaves finely. Heat 2 tbsps oil in a large pan and fry the vegetables gently. • Break up the tomatoes and add them to the vegetables together with their juice. Boil for a few minutes to reduce the liquid. • Heat the oven to 220°C/425°F/Gas Mark 7. •Rinse the sliced aubergine with cold water and pat dry. Heat the remaining oil in a separate pan and fry the aubergine until brown, then drain off any remaining oil. • Butter a large ovenproof dish and put in half the bucatini. Stir in 2 tbsps of the grated cheese and pour over the tomato sauce. Arrange the aubergine slices on top, then add the remaining bucatini, followed by another layer of aubergine. • Cover with thin slices of Mozzarella and bake for 30 minutes.

Gruyère Pasta au Gratin

4l/7 pints water
400g/14oz pasta,(bucatini,
tagliatelle or fusilli)
2 tsps salt
1 tbsp oil
400g/14oz Gruyère cheese
250ml/9fl oz whipping cream
Pinch each of salt and freshly
grated nutmeg
1 egg yolk
2 tbsps butter
2 tbsps chopped fresh parsley

Preparation time:
25 minutes
Baking time:
30 minutes
Nutritional value:
Analysis per serving, approx:
• 4200kJ/1000kcal
• 42g protein
• 59g fat
• 74g carbohydrate

• Grate the cheese. Whip the cream with the salt and nutmeg until it is reasonably thick. Mix in the egg yolk. • Butter an ovenproof dish. Place alternate layers of pasta and cheese in the dish, covering the top layer of pasta with the cream. Top with dabs of the remaining butter. • Place the dish on the middle shelf of a cold oven. Bake for 30 minutes at 200°C/400°F/ Gas Mark 6 until golden brown. • Before serving, garnish with parsley. • Serve with a green salad.

Tip: Instead of Gruyère, Emmental or Gouda may be used.

Bring the water to the boil. Add the pasta, the salt and oil. Cook the pasta until al dente, then drain in a colander.

Braised Courgettes

800g / 1¾lbs small courgettes
2 cloves garlic
1 tsp salt
¼ tsp black pepper
100g / 4oz streaky bacon
2 tbsps olive oil
125ml / 4 fl oz hot vegetable stock
1 tbsp chopped fresh sage or 1 tsp dried sage
6 tbsps single cream
Pinch of hot paprika
2 tbsps chopped chives

Preparation time:
30 minutes
Cooking time:
20 minutes
Nutritional value:
Analysis per serving, approx:
• 1365kJ/325kcal
• 6g protein
• 27g fat
• 14g carbohydrate

Wash and dry the courgettes, remove the stalk ends and cut into 2cm/¾-inch cubes. Peel and chop the garlic, and crush with the salt and pepper. Mix the courgettes in a bowl with the garlic. • Dice the bacon, fry in the oil and remove, using a slotted spoon. • Sauté the diced courgettes in the oil, browning on all sides. Add the vegetable stock and sage and braise, covered, over a gentle heat for 15 minutes. • Combine the paprika and the cream, mix into the courgettes, and continue cooking, uncovered, over a low heat to reduce the liquid. • Serve the courgettes sprinkled with the diced bacon and chopped chives. • This goes well with potato croquettes.

Our Tip: Use diced lean ham or 200g/7oz diced cooked chicken instead of the bacon. This would reduce the calorie count by about 420kJ/110kcal.

Broad Beans in Béchamel Sauce

1½kg/3lbs 6oz broad beans
(fresh or frozen)
500ml/16 fl oz vegetable stock
2 sprigs savory
25g/1oz butter
1 tbsp flour
1 small onion
½ bay leaf
2 cloves
Pinch each of salt, pepper and
grated nutmeg
125ml/4 fl oz single cream
1 tsp anchovy paste
2 tbsps chopped parsley

Preparation time:
15 minutes
Cooking time:
1 hour
Nutritional value:
Analysis per serving, approx:
• 1220kJ/290kcal
• 12g protein
• 15g fat
• 26g carbohydrate

Shell the beans, rinse in cold water and drain. Bring the vegetable stock to the boil with the savory. Add the beans, and cook, covered, for 30 minutes. • Drain the beans, reserving 375ml/⅝pint of the cooking liquid. • Melt the butter. Sprinkle in the flour, and stir until pale yellow, then gradually add the cooking liquid. • Peel the onion, stick the bay leaf and cloves into it, and place it in the sauce. Let the sauce simmer for 30 minutes, stirring frequently. • Remove the onion, and season to taste with salt, pepper and nutmeg. Combine the cream and anchovy paste, then mix into the sauce. Lastly add the broad beans to the sauce. • Serve sprinkled with parsley.

Green Beans
with Crème Fraîche

800g/1¾lbs French or runner
beans
1 onion
1 clove garlic
2 medium-sized carrots
2 tbsps corn oil
125ml/4 fl oz hot vegetable
stock
2 sprigs savory
1 tsp arrowroot
4 tbsps crème fraîche
2 tsps chopped fresh thyme or
1 tsp dried thyme

Preparation time:
20 minutes
Cooking time:
10–20 minutes
Nutritional value:
Analysis per serving, approx:
• 775kJ/185kcal
• 7g protein
• 10g fat
• 19g carbohydrate

Top and tail the beans,
stringing them if necessary,
and wash. Halve or quarter
large beans. Peel and chop the
onion and garlic very finely.
Scrape, wash and finely dice
the carrots. • Heat the oil and
sauté the onion and garlic in it.
Add the beans and diced carrot
and quickly toss in the fat. Top
up with the vegetable stock,
and add the savory. Cook for
10–20 minutes depending on
the thickness of the beans. •
Dissolve the arrowroot in 1
tbsp cold water, and mix with
the crème fraîche. Use this to
thicken the sauce. Remove the
savory. Sprinkle the thyme
over the vegetables. • Green
Beans with Crème Fraîche
makes a good accompaniment
for lamb chops and jacket
potatoes.

Chicory Fritters

8 medium-sized heads of
chicory
2 lemons
2 l/3½ pints water
2 tsps salt
150g/5 ½oz flour
2 eggs
125ml/4 fl oz lager
1 tsp salt
1 tsp sugar
A bunch of parsley
1l/1¾ pints oil for deep-frying

Preparation time:
20 minutes
Cooking time:
10 minutes
Nutritional value:
Analysis per serving, approx:
• 1720kJ/410kcal
• 11g protein
• 24g fat
• 37g carbohydrate

Remove the outer leaves of chicory and trim the stems. Squeeze the lemons. • Add the salt and lemon juice to the water and bring to the boil. Add the chicory heads and boil for 10 minutes. • Drain well, and allow to cool. Wash the parsley and shake dry. • To make the batter, sift the flour into a bowl. Separate the eggs. Combine the egg yolks, beer, salt and sugar with the flour. • Heat the oil to 180°C/350°F in a deep-fryer or chip pan. • Beat the egg whites until stiff, and fold into the batter. • Coat the heads of chicory, a few at a time, with the batter, and fry in the hot oil until crisp and brown, turning from time to time. Lift out of the oil using a slotted spoon, and leave on absorbent kitchen paper to drain. Make sure the temperature of the oil reaches 180°C/350°F each time before putting in more fritters. • Keep the chicory fritters warm on a preheated serving plate. Put the parsley into the hot fat for 2-3 minutes, drain and use to garnish the fritters. • These go well with potato and herring salad or fried sliced ham.

Leek Flan

Ingredients for a 26cm/10-inch flan (10 slices):

For the dough:
250g/8oz plain flour, sifted
Pinch of salt
1 egg
100g/4oz butter, cut into small pieces

For the filling:
600g/1lb 6oz leeks
200g/7oz streaky bacon
1 tbsp oil
Pinch of curry powder
200g/7oz mortadella
2 eggs
250ml/8 fl oz sour cream
Salt and black pepper

Preparation time:
15 minutes
Standing time:
1 hour
Cooking time:
45 minutes
Nutritional value:
Analysis per slice, approx:
• 1720kJ/410kcal
• 12g protein
• 31g fat
• 21g carbohydrate

To make the dough, knead the sifted flour, salt, egg and butter together. Cover and leave in the refrigerator to rest for 1 hour. • Slit the leeks in half lengthways, wash thoroughly, cut off the dark green ends and the roots, and slice the remaining white part. • Dice the bacon, and fry in the oil until golden. Add the leeks, season with salt, pepper and curry powder, cover, and braise over a low heat for 10 minutes. • Preheat the oven to 200°C/400°F/Gas Mark 6. • Roll out the dough, and use it to line the base and sides of a 26cm/10-inch springform tin. Pierce the pastry in several places with a fork. Dice the mortadella and distribute the pieces over the dough, then add the leek mixture. Beat the eggs, sour cream, salt and pepper together, and pour the mixture over the leeks. • Bake the flan on the middle shelf of the oven for 45 minutes.

Tomato and Crème Fraîche Flan

Ingredients for a 26cm/10-inch flan (8 slices):
200g/7oz frozen puff dough
600g/1lb 6oz tomatoes
3 eggs
¼ tsp each salt and white pepper
½ tsp freshly chopped basil
5 tbsps crème fraîche
15g/½oz butter, melted
5 tbsps freshly grated Cheddar cheese

Preparation time including thawing time:
40 minutes
Cooking time:
33 minutes
Nutritional value:
Analysis per slice, approx:
• 860kJ/205kcal
• 8g protein
• 14g fat
• 12g carbohydrate

Unwrap the frozen dough and leave to defrost; then roll out into a circle on a floured work surface. • Rinse a 26cm/10-inch springform tin in cold water. Lay the dough in the tin, raising the edge slightly to make a rim. Leave to rest in the refrigerator for 30 minutes. Preheat the oven to 200°C/400°F/Gas Mark 6. • Remove the hard stalk ends from the tomatoes, pour boiling water over them, skin and cut into small pieces. Arrange the tomatoes on the pastry base. Beat the eggs with the salt, pepper and basil. Gradually stir in the crème fraîche and the melted butter. Pour this mixture over the tomatoes, and sprinkle the grated cheese over the filling. • Cook on the middle shelf of the oven for 8 minutes. Lower the heat to 180°C/350°F/Gas Mark 4, and cook for up to another 25 minutes until golden brown. • If the topping becomes too brown before the flan is cooked, cover it with greaseproof paper or aluminium foil. • Serve piping hot.

Chinese Stir-fry Vegetables

8 dried Chinese mushrooms
(cloud ears)
500ml/16 fl oz hot water
4 spring onions
300g/10oz celery
300g/10oz carrots
300g/10oz red peppers
150g/5½oz each canned
bamboo shoots and bean
sprouts
1 small clove garlic
1 small piece fresh root ginger
(about 20g/¾oz)
5 tbsps sesame oil
4 tbsps soy sauce
½ tsp salt
¼ tsp each sugar and black
pepper

Preparation time:
40 minutes
Cooking time:
15 minutes
Nutritional value:
Analysis per serving, approx:
• 1010kJ/2405kcal
• 6g protein
• 14g fat
• 22g carbohydrate

Soak the dried mushrooms in the hot water for 30 minutes allowing them to swell. • Prepare the spring onions, celery and carrots, wash and cut into julienne strips. Halve the peppers, remove the pith and seeds, wash and cut into thin strips. Slice the bamboo and bean sprouts thinly; cut the bamboo shoots into small slices. Peel, chop and crush the garlic. Peel and grate the ginger. • Heat the oil in a wok or large frying-pan. Sauté the garlic, ginger and onion. • Reserve 125ml/4 fl oz of the water in which the mushrooms have been soaked. Squeeze excess moisture out of the mushrooms, and quarter them. • Add the celery, carrots and mushrooms to the vegetables in the wok, and cook for 4 minutes. • Pour the reserved soaking water over the vegetables. Add the pepper, and cook for a further 6 minutes or until the vegetables are tender. • Season well with the soy sauce, salt, sugar and

pepper. Mix in the bamboo
sprouts and bean shoots. • Heat
through for another 3 minutes.
• Chinese noodles and
medallions of pork make a
good accompaniment.

53

Neapolitan Vegetable Casserole

500g/1lb 2oz aubergines
2 tsps salt
2 yellow peppers
4 beefsteak tomatoes
600g/1lb 6oz potatoes
2 large onions
2 cloves garlic
125ml/4 fl oz olive oil
4 leaves fresh basil
1 tsp salt
¼ tsp black pepper
2 tbsps chopped chives

Preparation time:
40 minutes
Cooking time:
40-50 minutes
Nutritional value:
Analysis per serving, approx:
• 2245kJ/535kcal
• 10g protein
• 33g fat
• 49g carbohydrate

Thinly peel the aubergines, halve lengthways, and cut the halves into 2cm/¾-inch strips. Sprinkle salt over the sliced aubergine, and leave covered for 30 minutes. • Preheat the oven to 200°C/400°F/Gas Mark 6. • Prepare the peppers and cut into strips. Pour boiling water over the tomatoes, skin and cut into chunks, removing the hard stalk ends. Peel the potatoes and cut into sticks about 2cm/¾ inch in diameter. Peel the onions, and cut them also into strips. Peel and finely chop the garlic. • Discard the liquid that has been drawn from the aubergines. • Heat the oil in a flameproof dish with a lid. Sauté the onion and garlic until transparent, and add the prepared vegetables. Shred the basil leaves, and stir them into the vegetables with the pepper and salt. • Cover the casserole and cook on the lowest shelf of the oven for about 40-50 minutes until done. • Scatter the chives on top before serving. • Smoked bratwurst or other smoked continental sausages taste good with this casserole.

Onions au Gratin, Swiss Style

600g/1lb 6oz each potatoes
and onions
1 tsp salt
½ tsp coarsely ground black
pepper
250ml/8 fl oz vegetable stock
125ml/4 fl oz cream
150g/6oz Gruyère cheese,
freshly grated
45g/1½ oz butter
1 tbsp chopped parsley

Preparation time:
45 minutes
Cooking time:
55 minutes
Nutritional value:
Analysis per serving, approx:
• 1955kJ/465kcal
• 17g protein
• 28g fat
• 36g carbohydrate

Preheat the oven to 220°C/
430°F/Gas Mark 7. Peel
the potatoes and onions and
slice thinly. • Arrange the
potato and onion slices in
alternating layers in an
ovenproof dish, seasoning each
layer with salt and pepper.
Pour the vegetable stock over
them. • Bake in the oven for
up to 40 minutes or until
tender. • Mix the cream and
grated cheese and pour this
mixture over the vegetables.
Put dabs of butter on top, and
continue cooking for up to
another 15 minutes until the
topping is golden. • Serve
sprinkled with the parsley. • A
fresh mixed salad makes a good
accompaniment.

Italian Celery Flan

Ingredients for a 26cm/10-inch
flan (12 slices):
For the dough:
200g/7oz plain flour
60g/2oz cooking fat
3/4 tsp salt
125ml/4 fl oz water (scant
measure)
For the filling:
700g/1½lbs celery
500ml/16 fl oz water
2 medium-sized onions
4 eggs
3 tbsps single cream
100g/4oz Parmesan cheese,
freshly grated
¼ tsp white pepper
Pinch each of grated nutmeg
and salt
Fat for greasing the tin

Preparation time:
30 minutes
Cooking time:
40 minutes
Nutritional value:
Analysis per slice, approx:
• 800kJ/190kcal
• 8g protein
• 10g fat
• 17g carbohydrate

Grease a 26cm/10-inch
springform tin. • Work
the flour, cooking fat, salt and
water into a smooth dough.
Roll out the pastry and line
the base and sides of the tin.
Leave in the refrigerator to rest
for at least 30 minutes.•
Preheat the oven to 220°C/
430°F/Gas Mark 7. • Trim the
celery, wash it, halve the stalks
lengthways and cut into small
pieces. Bring the salted water
to the boil, and cook the
celery for 8 minutes. Peel and
finely chop the onions. • Drain
the celery. Beat the eggs with
the cream. Stir in the pieces of
celery, the chopped onion and
the Parmesan cheese. Season
liberally with pepper, nutmeg
and salt. Pour the mixture into
the pastry base. • Bake on the
middle shelf of the oven for 40
minutes. • Serve piping hot.

Greek Spinach Pie

Ingredients for 10 slices:
300g/10oz filo dough sheets
1kg/2¼lbs spinach
1l/1¾ pints water
1 tsp salt
1 bunch spring onions or 5 shallots
1 clove garlic
50g/2oz butter
¼ tsp each salt and white pepper
Pinch of grated nutmeg
200g/7oz Feta cheese
4 eggs
5 tbsps fresh breadcrumbs
1 egg yolk
Melted butter

Preparation time:
1 hour
Cooking time:
50 minutes
Nutritional value:
Analysis per slice, approx:
• 1175kJ/280kcal
• 14g protein
• 16g fat
• 19g carbohydrate

Defrost the phyllo dough. •
Pick over the spinach,
then wash it. Bring the salted
water to the boil. Blanch the
spinach for 4 minutes, drain
and chop coarsely. • Peel and
finely chop the spring onions
or shallots and the garlic, and
sauté in the melted butter until
transparent. Add the spinach.
Season the vegetables. • Dice
the cheese. Beat the eggs, and
mix into the spinach with the
breadcrumbs and cheese . •
Preheat the oven to 200°C/
400°F/Gas Mark 6. Rinse a
baking sheet in cold water. •
Defrost the dough, if frozen.
Cut out 6 rectangles measuring
25x30cm/10x12 inches. Brush
3 sheets of dough with melted
butter and arrange over half of
the baking sheet so that they
overlap the edge. Arrange the
spinach on top and fold the
overhanging edges in to the
centre to partially cover the
filling. Brush the remaining
sheets of dough with melted
butter and lay them on top;
pierce several holes in the
pastry lid with the tines of a
fork. Brush the top of the pie
with more melted butter and
the beaten egg yolk, and bake
for 50 minutes or until golden.

Buckwheat Spaghetti with Tofu Ragout

300g/10oz tofu (soya bean curd)
2 tbsps soya sauce
3 tbsps whole sesame seeds
Freshly ground black pepper
500g/1lb 2oz peeled plum tomatoes
500g/1lb 2oz cucumber
1 onion
4 tbsps oil
4l/7 pints water
2 tsps salt
400g/14oz buckwheat spaghetti
100g/4oz Pecorino or Parmesan cheese
250ml/9fl oz sour cream
4 tbsps finely chopped fresh dill
1 tsp paprika

Preparation and cooking time:
1 hour
Nutritional value:
Analysis per serving, approx:
• 2930kJ/710kcal
• 29g protein
• 30g fat
• 81g carbohydrate

Drain the tofu, cut into 5mm/¼-inch cubes, then place in a small bowl and marinate briefly in the soya sauce, the sesame seeds and the pepper. • Dice the tomatoes; dice the cucumber and onion. • Heat the oil in a large saucepan, add the onion and cook until transparent. Add the tofu and the marinade and cook for 2-3 minutes, stirring frequently. Then add the diced cucumber and tomato. Cook over a low heat for 10-15 minutes. • Bring the water to the boil, add the salt and cook the spaghetti until al dente. Drain in a colander, rinse briefly with cold water and place in a large, heated dish. • Grate the cheese coarsely. •

Remove the sauce from the heat, stir in the grated cheese, the sour cream and the dill, then season to taste with the paprika and perhaps some more soya sauce. • Serve the spaghetti topped with the sauce.

Aubergine Pizza

Ingredients for a 30cm/12-inch
flan (8 slices):
For the dough:
200g/7oz flour
15g/½oz fresh yeast or
8g/¼oz dried yeast
125ml/4 fl oz lukewarm water
1 tbsp olive oil
½ tsp salt
For the filling:
300g/10oz fillet of beef
2 tbsps olive oil
1 tsp fines herbes
2 cloves garlic
600g/1¼lbs aubergines
300g/10oz tomatoes
Salt and white pepper
100g/4oz Pecorino cheese,
freshly grated
15g/½oz butter
Olive oil for the dish

**Preparation time including
standing time:**
1 hour
Cooking time:
30 minutes
Nutritional value:
Analysis per slice, approx:
• 1090kJ/260kcal
• 15g protein
• 11g fat
• 25g carbohydrate

Make a yeast dough with the ingredients following the instructions given for the Onion Flan. • Cut the fillet of beef into strips 1cm/½ inch wide, and marinate in the olive oil with the herbs in a covered dish for 20 minutes. • Peel, chop and crush the cloves of garlic. Slice the aubergines and tomatoes. • Preheat the oven to 200°C/400°F/Gas Mark 6. Grease a 30cm/12-inch flan tin. • Roll out the yeast dough and use it to line the tin, raising the sides to form a shallow rim. • Arrange the strips of beef and the sliced aubergines and tomatoes on the pizza base. Sprinkle salt, pepper and crushed garlic on top, and sprinkle with the oil in which the meat has marinated. Scatter the cheese over the pizza and dot with butter. • Bake in the oven for 30 minutes.

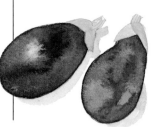

Artichoke Pizza

Ingredients for a 30cm/12-inch
flan tin (8 slices):
For the dough:
200g/7oz flour
15g/½oz fresh yeast or
8g/¼oz dried yeast
125ml/4 fl oz lukewarm water
1 tbsp olive oil
Pinch of salt
For the filling:
300g/10oz canned tuna
1 small clove garlic
½ tsp salt
1 tbsp olive oil
1 tsp dried thyme
¼ tsp white pepper
16 artichoke hearts
2 tbsps small capers
5 tbsps freshly grated Parmesan
2 egg yolks
3 tbsps crème fraîche
Olive oil to grease the tin

**Preparation time including
standing time:**
1 hour
Cooking time:
30 minutes
Nutritional value:
Analysis per slice, approx:
• 1325kJ/315kcal
• 16g protein
• 15g fat
• 29g carbohydrate

Preheat the oven to 200°C/
400°F/Gas Mark 6. Make a
yeast dough with the
ingredients, following the
instructions given for the
Onion Flan . • Drain the tuna
and break into pieces. Peel and
finely chop the garlic, sprinkle
salt over it and crush it. Mix it
with the olive oil, dried thyme
and pepper and pour this over
the tuna. Cut the artichoke
hearts into quarters. • Grease
the dish with oil. • Roll out
the dough into a circle and use
it to line a 30cm/12-inch flan
tin, raising the sides to form a
shallow rim. Arrange the
artichoke hearts over it, and
scatter the capers and pieces of
tuna on top. Combine the
cheese, egg yolks and crème
fraîche, and pour over the dish.
• Bake for 30 minutes.

Tagliatelle with Vegetables and Herb Paste

4 onions
250g/8oz courgettes
2 green peppers
250g/8oz mushrooms
2 beefsteak tomatoes
7 tbsps cold-pressed olive oil
1 tsp chicken stock granules
2 sprigs of tarragon
Handful each of fresh parsley, dill and basil
6 sage leaves
2 garlic cloves
2 tbsps almond leaves
Salt and freshly ground black pepper
1 tbsp lemon juice
300g/10oz tagliatelle
3l/5¼ pints water
1½ tsps salt

Preparation and cooking time:
1 hour
Nutritional value:
Analysis per serving, approx:
• 2100kJ/500kcal
• 16g protein
• 17g fat
• 73g carbohydrate

Peel the onions, cut in half lengthways and then into strips. Trim the courgettes, cut in half and slice. Remove the stalk, pith and seeds from the peppers and cut the flesh into pieces. Wipe the mushrooms, cutting the larger ones in half. Peel and dice the tomatoes, removing the seeds and the bases of the stalks. • Heat 4 tbsps oil. First add the onions and fry until transparent, then add all the chopped vegetables except the tomatoes and continue to cook for a further 5 minutes. • Sprinkle over the vegetable stock granules and some pepper, cover, and simmer over a low heat for 10 minutes. • Wash and dry the herbs, remove the stalks and chop finely. Peel and crush the garlic cloves and combine with the herbs, together with the crushed almond leaves. Stir in some salt, pepper, the lemon juice and the remaining olive oil. • Add the tomatoes to the

other vegetables. Continue cooking for a few minutes without a lid in order to reduce the liquid. • Cook the pasta in the salted water for about 8 minutes or until al dente, then drain; serve with the ragout and the herb paste.

Index